# Exploring Pyramids Around the World

## Making Models of Geometric Solids

Orli Zuravicky

# PowerMath™

The Rosen Publishing Group's
## PowerKids Press™
New York

Published in 2004 by The Rosen Publishing Group, Inc.
29 East 21st Street, New York, NY 10010

Book Design: Michael Tsanis

Photo Credits: Cover © Peter Adams/Index Stock; cover (inset) © Scott Goff/Index Stock; p. 7 © Kenneth
Garrett/National Geographic; p. 8 © Vladimir Pcholkin/Taxi; p. 11 © Richard T. Nowitz/Corbis; p. 14 ©
W. Cody/Corbis; p. 15 © Jonathan Blair/Corbis; p. 19 © Roger Wood/Corbis; p. 23 © Sergio Pitamitz/Corbis;
p. 24 © Charles & Josette Lenars/Corbis; p. 27 © Craig Lovell/Corbis; p. 30 (pencil) by Maura B. McConnell.

Library of Congress Cataloging-in-Publication Data

Zuravicky, Orli.
  Exploring pyramids around the world : making models of geometric
solids / Orli Zuravicky.
       v. cm. — (PowerMath)
Includes index.
Contents: What is a 3-dimensional model? — The history of pyramids —
The great pyramid at Giza — Pyramids of Nubia — The step pyramid —
The pyramids of Central America — The Transamerica building — Seeing
the world in 3-D.
  ISBN 0-8239-8992-5 (lib. bdg.)
  ISBN 0-8239-8908-9 (pbk.)
  ISBN 0-8239-7436-7 (6-pack)
  1. Pyramid (Geometry)—Juvenile literature. 2.  Models and
modelmaking—Juvenile literature. 3.  Pyramids—Juvenile literature. [1.
Pyramid (Geometry) 2. Models and modelmaking. 3. Pyramids. 4. Shape.]
I. Title. II. Series.
  QA491.Z87 2004
  516'.15—dc21

                                    2003001011

Manufactured in the United States of America

# Contents

What Is a 3-Dimensional Model?                                    4

The History of Pyramids                                          6

The Great Pyramid at Giza                                       10

The Pyramids of Nubia                                           14

The Step Pyramid                                               18

The Pyramids of Central America                                22

The Transamerica Building                                      26

Seeing the World in 3-D                                        30

Glossary                                                      31

Index                                                        32

# What Is a 3-Dimensional Model?

Sometimes it's hard to imagine how something looks without seeing it in front of you. **Architects** make drawings and models of the buildings they **design** before they are built. These models help them make the buildings properly, so that the buildings will stand straight and last for a long time.

Anyone can build a model. Models help us to understand things about a shape that a drawing can't show us. Throughout this book, you will learn about the **pyramids** all around the world, what they were made of, and how you can build your own models of famous pyramids!

Flat shapes, like a triangle or a square, have 2 measurable **dimensions**: length and width. They are called 2-dimensional, or 2-D, shapes. A cube

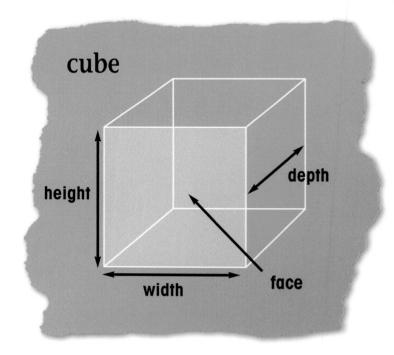

cube

height

width

depth

face

is a 3-dimensional, or 3-D, shape. The dimensions of a 3-D shape are known as **height**, width, and **depth**. Height is the distance from the top to the bottom of an object. Depth is the distance from the front to the back of an object.

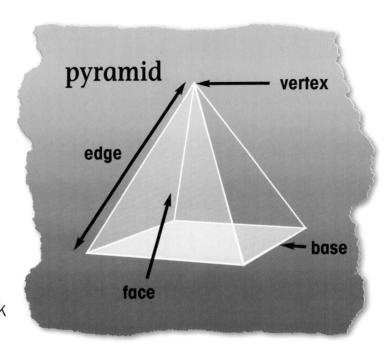

A pyramid is also a 3-dimensional shape. Pyramids, cubes, and most other 3-D shapes have sides called faces. Faces are flat surfaces that meet at the edges of the shape. The point, or corner, where 3 or more edges meet is called a **vertex**. The base is the bottom of the object. In order to create a 3-D model of a shape, you need to know how many faces it has and the shapes of its faces and its base.

# The History of Pyramids

The pyramids of ancient Egypt have amazed people for thousands of years. Egypt is a country in Africa and was home to one of the oldest civilizations in the world. How did the ancient Egyptians build such enormous structures? What was the purpose of the pyramids? Over the years, many people have tried to figure out the answers to these questions.

The earliest pyramids were built around 2600 B.C. That's about 4,600 years ago! The pyramids were built as **tombs** for ancient Egyptian rulers and court officials. Ancient Egyptians believed that a person's soul, which they called the *ka,* continued to live after the body died. They filled the pyramids with treasures and everyday things that they believed the dead person would need in the next life. Rulers were buried in their great pyramids with gold, furniture, clothing, and other things they would need in the next world.

The burial chambers of many of the ancient pyramids were built to look like the inside of a royal palace so the ruler's spirit would feel at home. Ancient Egyptian writing often covered the walls and doors of the burial chambers.

pyramid at
Teotihuacan, Mexico

Although the Egyptian pyramids are the most famous, there are many pyramids in Mexico and **Central America** as well. These pyramids were built centuries after the Egyptian pyramids as temples for honoring gods.

The Maya, Aztecs, and other Native Americans built huge pyramids in Mexico and Central America. Many of these pyramids were topped by temples where religious **ceremonies** took place. The pyramids of Mexico and Central America were made with many different kinds of stone, while Egyptian pyramids were made only from **limestone**.

Different civilizations built different types of pyramids. Scientists can tell many things about a civilization just by studying its pyramids. Now that we know a little bit about the history of pyramids, let's explore some famous pyramids around the world!

The pyramids in the ancient city of Teotihuacan, Mexico, are still standing after thousands of years!

# The Great Pyramid at Giza

Three of the world's most famous pyramids stand at a place in Egypt called Giza (GEE-zuh), near the city of Cairo (KY-roh). All 3 pyramids were built for famous Egyptian kings. One of these pyramids is called the Great Pyramid. It is the largest and most famous pyramid ever built! It was built for King Khufu (KOO-foo), who ruled Egypt around 2500 B.C.

The Great Pyramid is around 4,500 years old and was about 480 feet tall when it was first built. The Great Pyramid was the tallest structure in the world for over 43 centuries. It is made from over 2 million blocks of limestone and weighs around 5,750,000 tons! The pyramid is almost solid stone, but inside there are some hidden rooms, including the burial place of King Khufu. Next to the Great Pyramid stand the smaller pyramids built for 2 later kings named Khafre (KA-fruh) and Menkaure (men-KUHR-uh).

The Grand Gallery was believed to be a holding place for the huge stone blocks that were later used to seal up the king's burial chamber to protect it from thieves.

# Great Pyramid

## inside the Great Pyramid

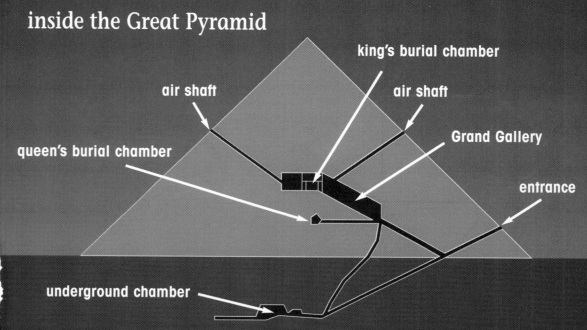

king's burial chamber

air shaft

air shaft

Grand Gallery

queen's burial chamber

entrance

underground chamber

# 3-dimensional model of the Great Pyramid

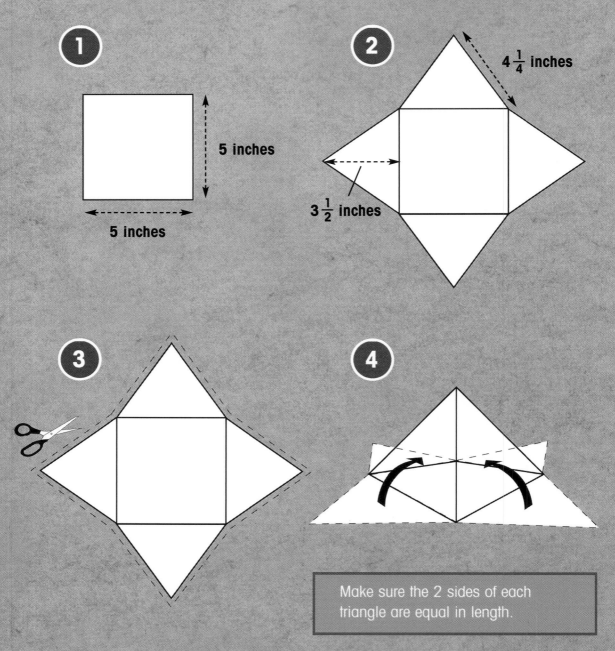

**1** 5 inches / 5 inches

**2** $4\frac{1}{4}$ inches / $3\frac{1}{2}$ inches

**3**

**4** Make sure the 2 sides of each triangle are equal in length.

Let's make a model of the Great Pyramid. The Great Pyramid has a square base and 4 triangular faces. Using a ruler, draw a big square (at least 5 inches on each side) in the middle of a large piece of heavy construction paper. This will be the base of our model pyramid. With the ruler, draw 4 triangles that are $3\frac{1}{2}$ inches tall, using the 4 edges of the square as bases for the triangles. These will be the faces of the pyramid. The sides of the triangles should be about $4\frac{1}{4}$ inches long.

Once you've drawn the base and all 4 faces of the pyramid, use scissors to cut along the edges of the 4 triangles. Don't cut the square base. Once you have cut the shape out, fold the 4 triangles up along the 4 lines of the square base. The triangles should meet each other at the top of the pyramid. Use tape to hold the 4 points together, and you have made a 3-dimensional, or 3-D, model of the Great Pyramid at Giza!

# The Pyramids of Nubia

South of Egypt is a place called Nubia (NOO-bee-uh). Today, Nubia is part of a country called Sudan. Long ago, the Nubians were neighbors of the ancient Egyptians. There are over 100 pyramids still standing in Nubia! Like the Egyptian pyramids, Nubian pyramids were also built as tombs for rulers and court officials. However, the Nubian pyramids were much smaller than the Egyptian pyramids, and their sides were much steeper. The Nubian pyramids had special temples built around them. The temples were places to pray and leave gifts to honor the dead rulers and officials who were buried inside the pyramids.

Some people believe that the pyramid shown on the U.S. $1.00 bill is not the Great Pyramid at Giza, but a Nubian pyramid built around 500 B.C.!

Nubian pyramids

# 3-dimensional model of a Nubian pyramid

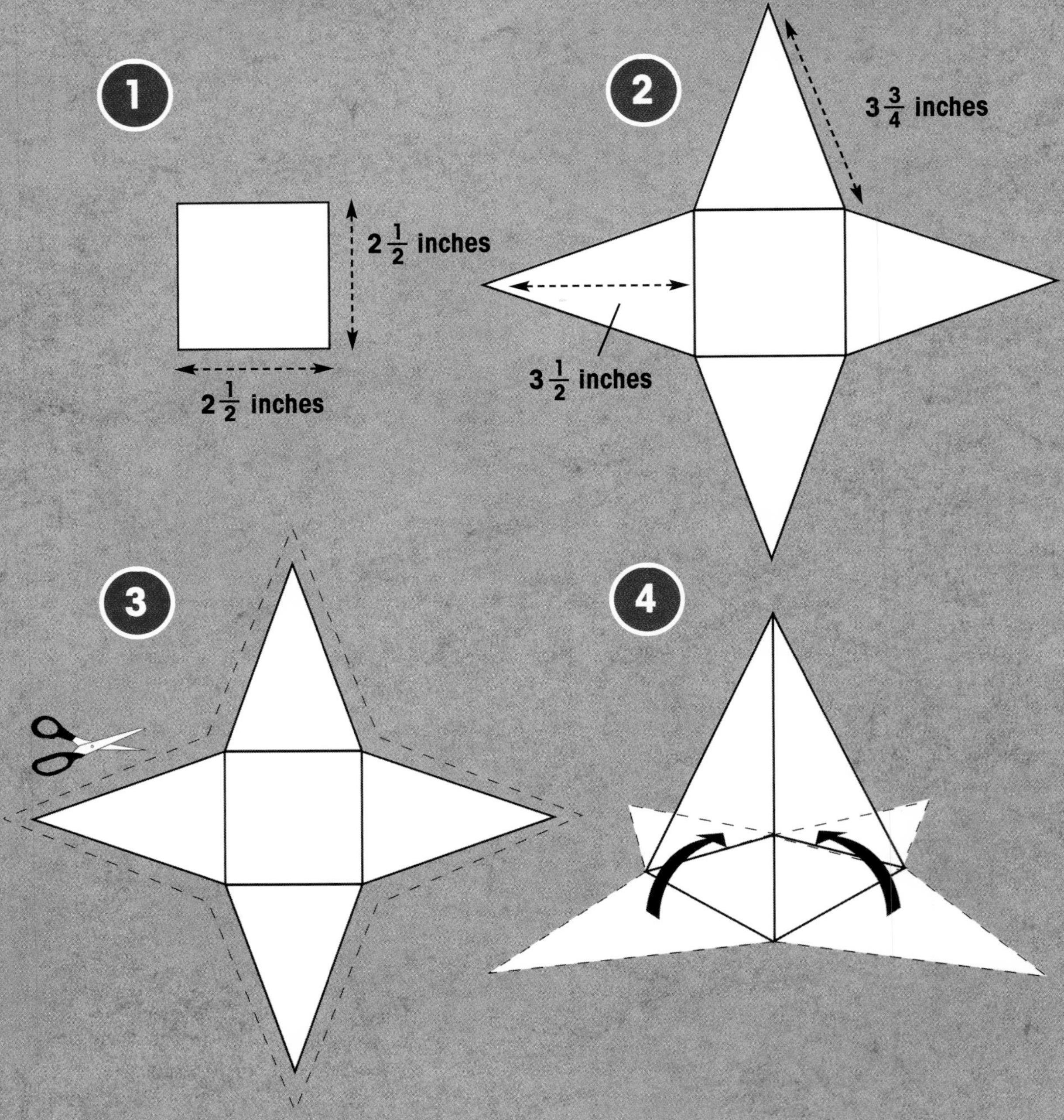

**1**

$2\frac{1}{2}$ inches

$2\frac{1}{2}$ inches

**2**

$3\frac{3}{4}$ inches

$3\frac{1}{2}$ inches

**3**

**4**

We can begin building a 3-D model of a Nubian pyramid the same way we began the model of the Great Pyramid, by drawing a square in the middle of a heavy sheet of paper. Make the square base for this pyramid smaller than the Great Pyramid base, about $2\frac{1}{2}$ inches on each side. Draw the 4 triangle faces as you did in the first model. The sides of the triangles should be $3\frac{3}{4}$ inches, and the heights should be $3\frac{1}{2}$ inches. Then cut, fold, and tape the same way you did with the first model.

The faces of the Nubian pyramid will be thinner than the faces of the Great Pyramid because the Nubian pyramids were steeper than the Egyptian pyramids.

# The Step Pyramid

The pyramid of King Khufu was the first true pyramid, which means it was the first pyramid to have smooth, sloping sides. However, the earliest known pyramid was built almost 200 years earlier by King Djoser (DJOH-suhr). Djoser's pyramid is known as the Step Pyramid because it looks like 6 giant steps. It was built near the Egyptian city of Saqqara (suh-KAHR-uh) around 2680 B.C.

A man named Imhotep (IHM-hoh-tep) designed the pyramid. Imhotep was Djoser's architect, doctor, and priest. His first design for Djoser's tomb was a large **mastaba**, which was the kind of tomb that had been used in Egypt for many years. The word "mastaba" means "bench." These ancient tombs looked like stone benches with sloping sides. Then Imhotep decided that Djoser's tomb needed to be larger and grander. He designed a tomb that looked like 6 mastabas stacked on top of each other. Each mastaba was smaller than the one below it. This made a pyramid shape.

King Djoser and some of his relatives were buried deep inside the Step Pyramid in small, secret rooms. The Egyptians hoped that robbers would not be able to find their way into the pyramid to steal the valuable things buried with the king.

Step Pyramid at Saqqara

# 3-dimensional model of King Djoser's Step Pyramid

1. 14 inches / 14 inches

2. 12 inches

To build your model of King Djoser's Step Pyramid, you will need several sheets of heavy paper.

On the first sheet, draw a square that is 14 inches on each side. Cut out the square. Now measure in 1 inch from each side of this square and draw a square that is 12 inches on each side. Draw lines to join the corners of the inner square to the outer corners. Cut along those lines. Now fold the edges under to form gently sloping sides. Tape the edges where the sloping sides meet. This will be the bottom mastaba, the largest one.

Repeat these steps to create the remaining mastabas, using a 12-inch square, an 10-inch square, an 8-inch square, a 6-inch square, and a 4-inch square. Stack the mastabas on top of each other, from largest to smallest, using tape to hold them together. You've created a 3-D model of the Step Pyramid!

# The Pyramids of Central America

Hundreds of years after the Nubians and Egyptians built their pyramids, people began building pyramids in Mexico and Central America. These pyramids were built by different Native American groups.

The Maya were a people who lived in southern Mexico and the parts of Central America that are now Guatemala, Belize, and Honduras, from around 200 A.D. to around 900 A.D. They used math and **astronomy** to design their pyramids. Many Mayan pyramids were built as bases for temples, and they looked very much like step pyramids. Their sides were steeper than the sides of Egyptian pyramids. Mayan pyramids were built from stone blocks and had staircases that the priests climbed to reach the temples at the top.

Tikal was an ancient city in Guatemala that was built by the Maya. Around the year 900, the Maya left the city for reasons that are still a mystery. Still standing at Tikal are many beautiful pyramids, temples, homes, and other Mayan buildings, as well as an area that resembles a modern soccer field.

pyramid at
Tikal, Guatemala

Aztec pyramid in Tenochtitlan

The Aztecs ruled a great empire in Mexico from the early 1400s until around 1520. Their capital city was located where Mexico City is today. The Aztecs were excellent farmers and warriors. Education was important to the Aztecs, and both boys and girls went to school to learn Aztec history and religion. Along with pyramids, the Aztecs created beautiful paintings, statues, and other types of art. The Aztecs also used a calendar much like the one we use today.

The Aztecs used their pyramids for religious ceremonies. These pyramids had 2 large staircases leading up to the temple at the top. The levels, or steps, of the pyramid are much taller than those of a Mayan pyramid, and there are fewer of them. Both Aztec and Mayan pyramids were much smaller than Egyptian pyramids.

This picture shows an Aztec pyramid in the ancient city of Tenochtitlan, near where Mexico City is today. Once you get used to making models, you can add Mayan and Aztec features like staircases and temples to your creations!

# The Transamerica Building

Today's buildings are much different than the pyramids that were built centuries ago. Modern building materials and machinery have allowed architects to create buildings that are taller and bigger than the pyramids of long ago. In 1968, a man named John Beckett gave the United States its very own pyramid. One day Beckett noticed how beautifully the Sun shone through the trees in a city park in San Francisco, California. He decided to create a building that would allow sunlight to reach the street below in the same way. Today, a modern pyramid stands in downtown San Francisco—the Transamerica Building. The Transamerica Building is made from stone, concrete, glass, and steel. It is 853 feet tall, almost twice the height of the Great Pyramid at Giza!

An estimated 10,000 to 100,000 people were needed to build the Great Pyramid, and it probably took about 30 years to build. Because of modern machinery and materials, the Transamerica Building was built in less than 3 years by only about 1,500 people.

Transamerica Building

# 3-dimensional model of the Transamerica Building

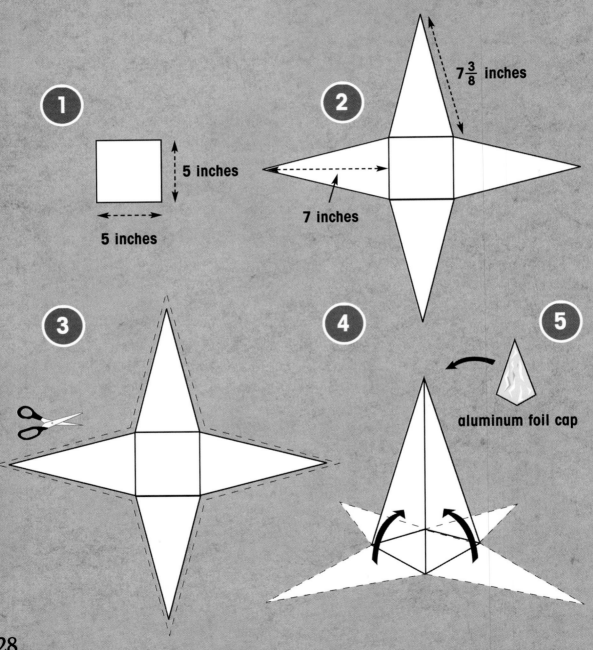

**1** 5 inches

5 inches

**2** 7 3/8 inches

7 inches

**3**

**4** aluminum foil cap

**5**

The Transamerica Building's shape means its 48 floors aren't of equal size. The largest floor is the 5th floor, which has 21,025 square feet. The 48th floor is the smallest, with 2,025 square feet. At the top of the building is the pyramid's tip, a 212-foot pointed roof covered in aluminum, a silver-colored metal that reflects the light from the Sun.

Make a basic 3-D model of the Transamerica Building by using the same instructions we used for the Great Pyramid. The Transamerica Building is steep like the Nubian pyramids, and its height is almost twice the height of the Great Pyramid, although its base is a little bit smaller. Following the Great Pyramid instructions, keep the base measurements the same, but double the height of the triangles. Finish by covering a small part of the top of the pyramid with aluminum foil to create the roof!

# Seeing the World in 3-D

Learning about places, civilizations, and buildings that are far away or existed in the distant past can be confusing. Some buildings look much different from the buildings we are familiar with. Others are too far away are to see in real life. Building **scale models** of these things lets us explore them.

Now that you have learned about the pyramids of the world by making 3-D models, think of all the other things you can build! You can make a model of the Sears Tower in Chicago, the Eiffel Tower in France, or the Empire State Building in New York City! By learning how to build models of these things, you'll learn their history, how they were built, how tall they are, and many other interesting facts about them. What kind of model would you like to build?

# Glossary

**architect** (AR-kuh-tekt)  A person who designs buildings.

**astronomy** (uh-STRAH-nuh-mee)  The study of the Sun, the Moon, planets, stars, and other space objects.

**Central America** (SEHN-truhl uh-MAIR-uh-kuh)  The land that connects Mexico to South America. Guatemala, El Salvador, Honduras, Nicaragua, Costa Rica, Panama, and Belize are in Central America.

**ceremony** (SAIR-uh-moh-nee)  An event to honor the importance of something.

**depth** (DEPTH)  The distance from the front to the back of an object.

**design** (dih-ZYNE)  To make a drawing that serves as a guide or plan.

**dimension** (duh-MEN-shun)  A measurement of height, length, width, or depth.

**height** (HITE)  The distance from the top to the bottom of an object.

**limestone** (LYME-stohn)  A rock formed from animal remains like shells and coral.

**mastaba** (MAH-stah-bah)  The earliest type of Egyptian tomb. It is shaped like a rectangular box with sloping sides.

**pyramid** (PEER-uh-mid)  A large structure that usually has a square or rectangular base and 4 triangular sides meeting in a point at the top.

**scale model** (SKAYL MAH-duhl)  A small, exact copy of something that has the same proportions as the original object.

**tomb** (TOOM)  A building where the dead are buried.

**vertex** (VUHR-teks)  The point, or corner, at which the edges of a shape meet.

# Index

**A**
Africa, 6
Aztec(s), 9, 25

**B**
Beckett, John, 26

**C**
Cairo, 10
Central America, 9, 22

**D**
Djoser, 18, 21

**E**
Egypt, 6, 10, 14, 18
Egyptian(s), 6, 9, 10, 14, 18,
    22, 25

**G**
Giza, 10, 13, 26
Great Pyramid, 10, 13, 17,
    26, 29

**I**
Imhotep, 18

**K**
Khafre, 10
Khufu, 10, 18

**M**
Maya(n), 9, 22, 25
Menkaure, 10
Mexico, 9, 22, 25
Mexico City, 25

**N**
Nubia, 14
Nubian(s), 14, 17, 22

**S**
San Francisco, California, 26
Saqqara, 18
Step Pyramid, 18, 21
Sudan, 14

**T**
temple(s), 9, 14, 22, 25
3-dimensional (3-D), 5, 13, 17,
    21, 29, 30
tomb(s), 6, 14, 18
Transamerica Building, 26, 29
2-dimensional (2-D), 5

**U**
United States, 26